Book 2

Your First Guitar Method

Mary Thompson

Chester Music
(A division of Music Sales Limited)
8/9 Frith Street, London W1V 5TZ

About Book 2

Following on from Book 1 in the series, this book will help you to develop your guitar skills one step at a time. In Book 1 you learned the names of the notes, and some of the signs and symbols used in music. In Book 2 you will learn more guitar techniques, and begin to play more than one note at a time.

Here are some reminders of the things you learned in Book 1. See how many you can remember.

This is a treble clef.

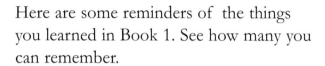

This tells you the music is written in tablature.

This is a semibreve, or whole note. It lasts for four beats.

This is a minim, or half note. It lasts for two beats.

This is a crotchet, or quarter note. It lasts for one beat.

This is a time signature.

This is a repeat sign.

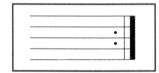

_P_ is short for _piano_. It means "play quietly".

This book © Copyright 1998 Chester Music.
Order No. CH61410   ISBN 0-7119-6791-1

Music and text setting by Mary Thompson
Illustrations by Nigel Hooper
Cover design by Ian Butterworth
Printed in the United Kingdom by Printwise (Haverhill) Limited, Haverhill, Suffolk.

Notes you have learned so far

Here is a reminder of all the notes you
learned in Book 1.

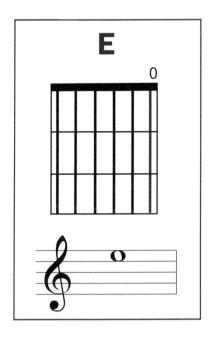

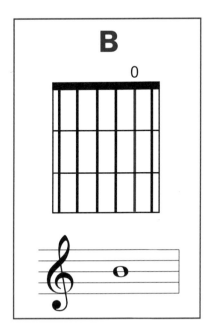

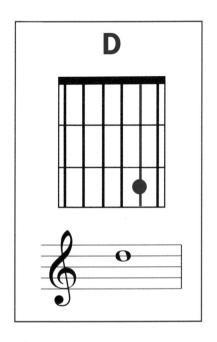

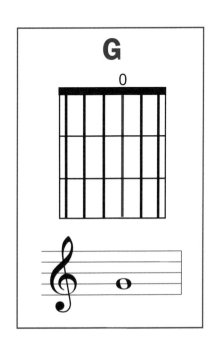

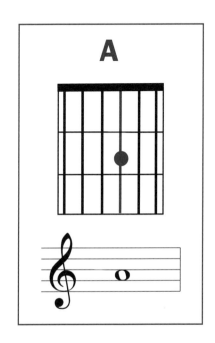

Playing loudly

In Book 1 you learned the Italian word *piano*, which means "quietly". Sometimes you have to play the music loudly. The Italian word for "loudly" is *forte*. The word *forte* is often shortened to *f*.

To play loudly, strike the strings harder, keeping your fingers a little more upright. Try playing a few notes, striking the strings harder for some. Listen to how loud or quiet each note sounds.

The picture on the right shows you how to play another D on your guitar.

This is where D is written on the stave.

See if you can spot this D in the next tune.

This D sounds lower than the D you learned in Book 1. Play both Ds. Can you hear the difference?

Shout It Out

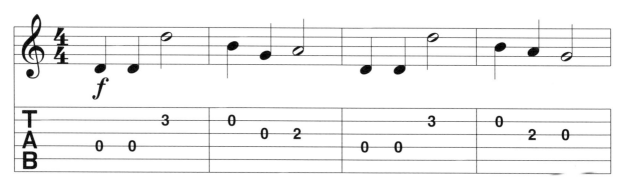

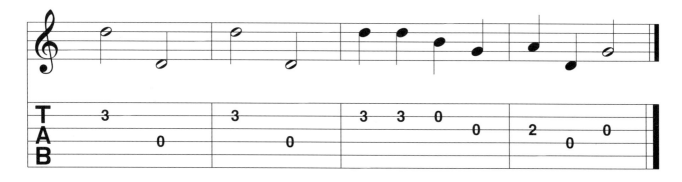

The picture on the right shows you how to play C on your guitar.

This is where C is written on the stave.

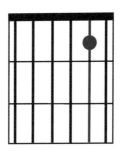

In the tune below, remember to play C using the first finger of your left hand.

See if you can spot this C in the next tune.

By The Sea

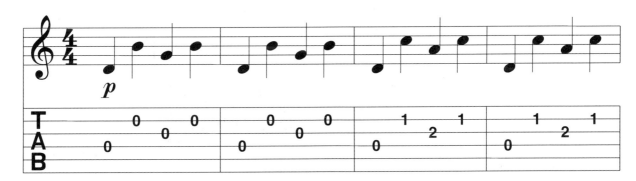

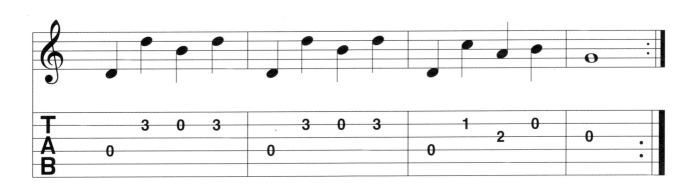

Remember to play "By The Sea" quietly.

Dotted notes

Sometimes there is a dot after a note. This makes the note last for one and a half times its normal length. For example, a minim lasts for two beats, so a minim with a dot after it lasts for three beats. When there is a dot after a note, it is called a dotted note.

This is a dotted minim. Dotted minims are also called dotted half notes.

Polka Dot Waltz

Remember to play this tune loudly.

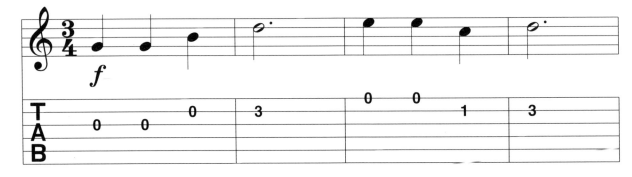

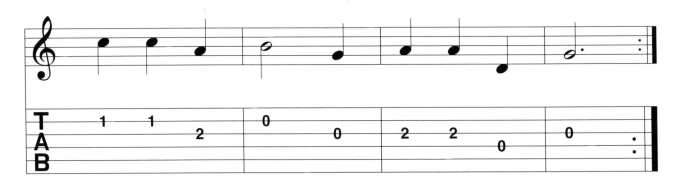

Leaving gaps in music

There are signs in music that tell you to leave gaps. These gaps are called rests. When you see a rest, count the correct number of beats in your head, before playing the next note.

A semibreve rest is also used to show a rest which lasts for a whole bar.

A crotchet (or quarter) rest = 1 beat

A minim (or half) rest = 2 beats

A semibreve (or whole) rest = 4 beats

Take A Break

To stop the strings from sounding during a rest, gently touch the strings with the side of your right hand. This is called damping the sound.

You can practise counting this rhythm by clapping the beats. Miss one clap for a crotchet rest and two claps for a minim rest.

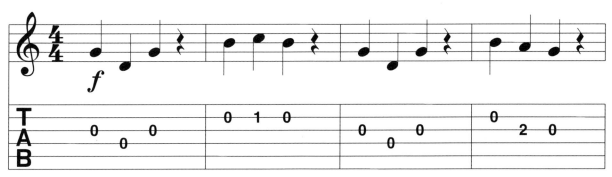

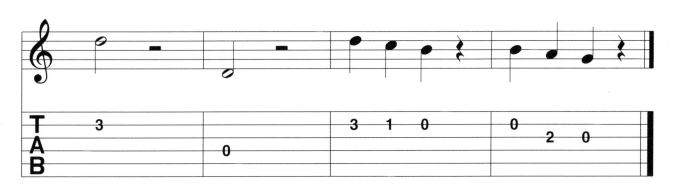

Using your right-hand fingers

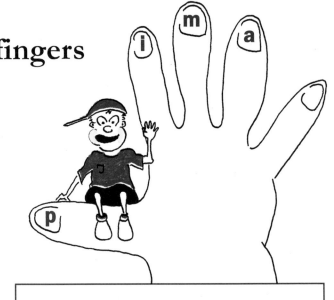

In Book 1 you learned to pluck the strings with your right-hand first finger, or a plectrum. As you learn to play more notes, you need to start using your first three fingers and thumb. This helps to make the music sound smooth. Use your thumb to play the bottom three strings and your fingers to play the top three strings.

Your right-hand fingers and thumb have special names in guitar music. These names are in Spanish. Usually they are shortened to the first letter of each word: p, i, m and a. You can see which letter goes with each finger on the right. You do not need to use your little finger in this book.

'P' stands for pulgar, which means "thumb"; 'i' stands for indicio, which means "index finger"; 'm' stands for medio, which means "middle finger", and 'a' stands for anular which means "ring finger".

Right On

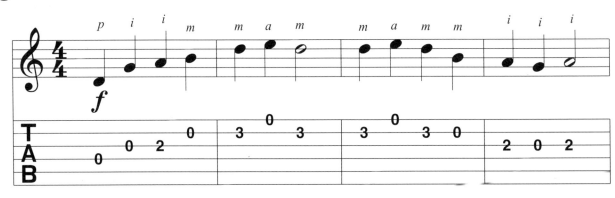

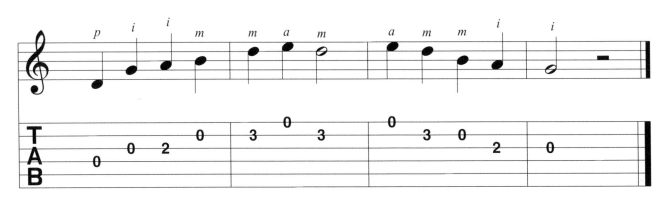

Using your left-hand fingers

When you are pressing a string with a left-hand finger, you do not always have to remove it straight away. Sometimes it is better to keep pressing it down until you need to remove it.

For example, in the tune below, you can keep your left-hand fingers down for the whole of the first two bars, and the fourth and fifth bars. This is much easier than removing them after each note.

The picture on the right shows you how to play F sharp on your guitar.

This is where F sharp is written on the stave.

A sharp sign in front of a note makes it slightly higher. The sharp sign also applies to any other Fs later in the same bar.

In the tune below, all the Fs are F sharps. Press down with the second finger of your left hand.

Stay Sharp

Remember, this note is F sharp too.

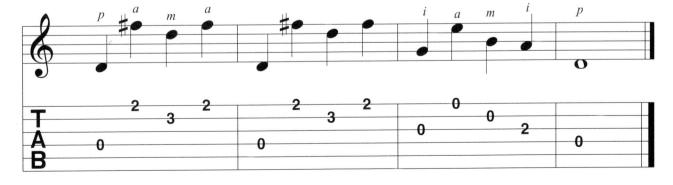

9

Playing two notes at the same time

So far you have only played one note at a
time. Now you will start playing two notes
together. Don't worry if you find it a bit
difficult at first. The more you practise,
the easier it will become. There are some
tips below to help you.

Read the tips
below before you
try "All Together".

All Together

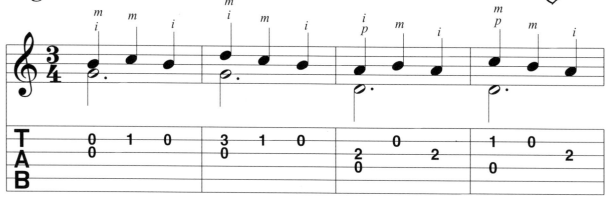

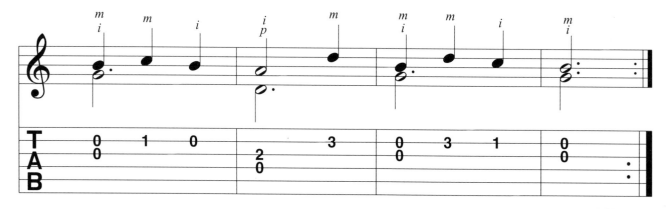

Practice hints

- Remember to use the correct
  fingers for each note.

- Try to pluck both strings at
  exactly the same time.

- Start off very slowly at first.
  When you are sure of the notes,
  gradually play the music faster
  until you are playing at a
  comfortable speed.

Another note-length

Here you are going to learn about a shorter note, called a quaver. A quaver lasts for half a crotchet beat. It looks like a crotchet with a tail.

Quavers are often joined together in groups of two or four. This makes them easier to read. You can see what they look like below.

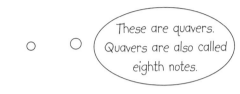

These are quavers. Quavers are also called eighth notes.

This is how two quavers are joined together.

This is how four quavers are joined together.

Quivering Quavers

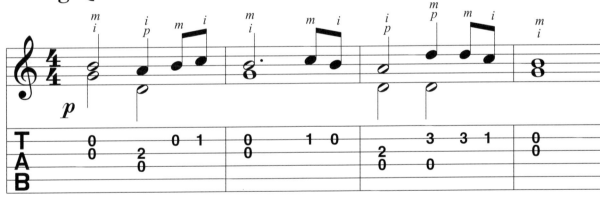

Dotted crotchets

A dotted crotchet lasts for one and a half crotchet beats. You can see what a dotted crotchet looks like on the right. To play dotted crotchets, it helps to count "one and two and". Before you play the next tune, try clapping the rhythm.

This is a dotted crotchet. Dotted crotchets are also called dotted half notes.

The picture on the right shows you how to play another A on your guitar.

This is where A is written on the stave.

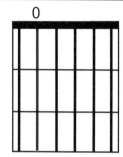

This A sounds lower than the A you learned in Book 1. Play both As and listen to the difference.

Can you spot both As in the next tune?

Medieval Magic

The picture on the right shows you
how to play another G on your guitar.

This is where
G is written
on the stave.

Can you spot both Gs in the next tune?

This G sounds higher than
the G you learned in Book 1.

Merry-go-round

Playing chords

Groups of two or more notes played at the same time are called chords. In guitar music, chords are often used to accompany melodies, especially in songs.

The chord you are going to learn here is called a D major chord. The name of the chord is often written as a letter above the music, instead of writing out all the notes.

The picture on the right shows you how to play a D major chord.

This is where the notes are written on the stave.

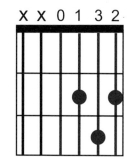

An x tells you not to play that string.

The numbers tell you which left-hand fingers to use.

Press down at the frets, as shown above, then play each string on its own to make sure you can hear all the notes clearly.

When you can hear all the notes clearly, run your right-hand thumb, or a plectrum, across the strings.

Major Player

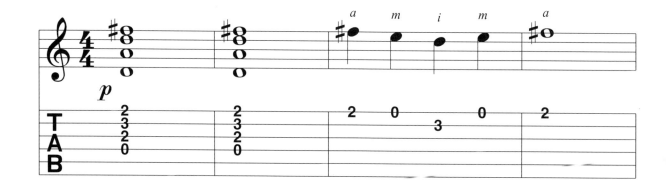

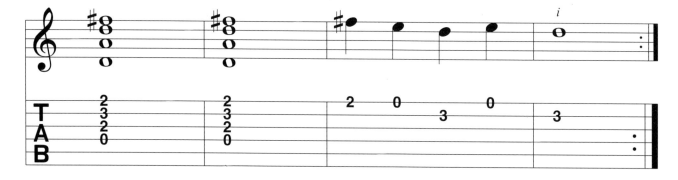

Tied notes

Sometimes the same notes are joined together by a curved line, called a tie. When notes are joined together like this, you add the number of beats together and play one long note. For example, if you see a semibreve tied to a minim, you play one note lasting for six beats.

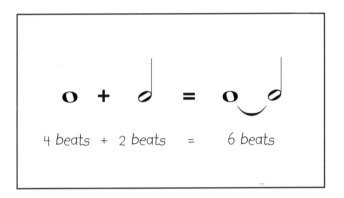

All Tied Up

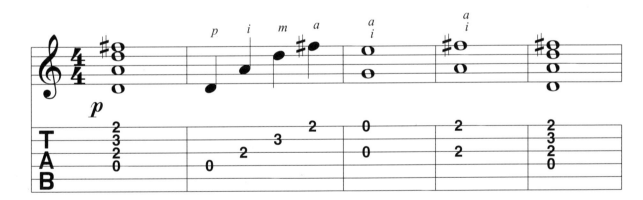

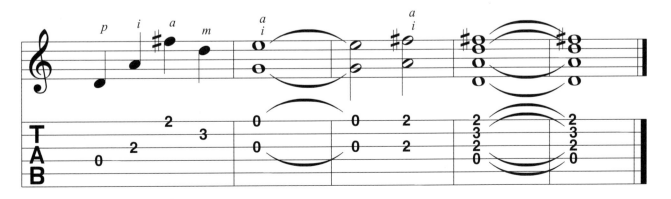

Congratulations!

Now that you have reached the end of the book, here is a special piece for you play. Practise it until you can play it all the way through without any mistakes. Then you can play it to a friend or relative, to show them what you have learned.

Farewell

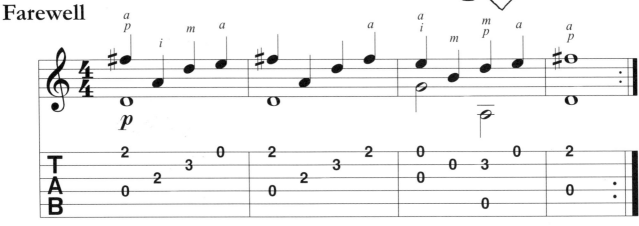

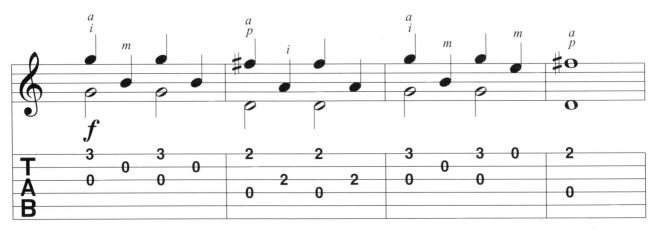

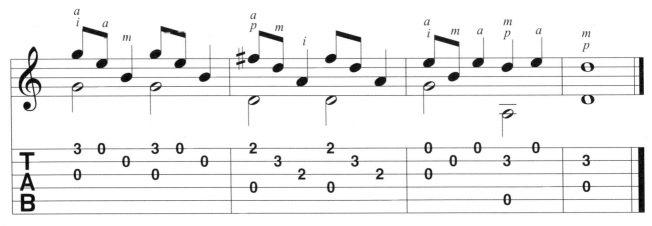

02/06 (57657)